T0087054

Yesterday, Today, and Tomorrow

Bob Chilcott

for SSA and piano

vocal score

OXFORD
UNIVERSITY PRESS

OXFORD
UNIVERSITY PRESS

Great Clarendon Street, Oxford OX2 6DP,
United Kingdom

Oxford University Press is a department of the University of Oxford.
It furthers the University's objective of excellence in research, scholarship,
and education by publishing worldwide. Oxford is a registered trade mark of
Oxford University Press in the UK and in certain other countries

© Oxford University Press 2023

Bob Chilcott has asserted his right under the Copyright, Designs
and Patents Act, 1988, to be identified as the Composer of this Work

All rights reserved. No part of this publication may be reproduced,
stored in a retrieval system, or transmitted, in any form or by any means,
without the prior permission in writing of Oxford University Press

Permission to perform this work in public (except in the course of divine worship)
should normally be obtained from a local performing right licensing organization,
unless the owner or the occupier of the premises being used already holds
a licence from such an organization. Likewise, permission to make and
exploit a recording of these works should be obtained from a
local mechanical copyright licensing organization

Enquiries concerning reproduction outside the scope of the above
should be directed to the Music Rights Department, Oxford University Press,
at music.permissions.uk@oup.com or at the address above

ISBN 978–0–19–356833–4

Music and text origination by Katie Johnston
Printed in Great Britain on acid-free paper by
Halstan & Co. Ltd, Amersham, Bucks.

Contents

1. Yesterday 5
2. Today 12
3. Tomorrow 19

Composer's note

In 1998 I wrote a piece for upper voices called *Look to this day!*, which included this inspiring Sanskrit text: 'Look to this day! For today well lived, makes every yesterday a dream of happiness, every tomorrow a vision of hope'. This text has stayed with me, and I suggested to the poet Georgia Way that she might use it as a starting point to write three texts for songs that express the past, the present, and the future. Georgia's poems not only translate the idea of this text in a striking and contemporary way, but also bring the energy and joy of youth to the fore. *Yesterday, Today, and Tomorrow* was written for the 2023 Crescent City Choral Festival and commissioned by the New Orleans Children's Chorus and their Director, Cheryl Dupont.

Duration: *c.*10 minutes

Commissioned by the New Orleans Children's Chorus and their Artistic Director, Cheryl Dupont, for the 2023 Crescent City Choral Festival

Yesterday, Today, and Tomorrow

1. Yesterday

Georgia Way (b. 1992)

BOB CHILCOTT

Music © Oxford University Press 2023. Text © Georgia Way. Reproduced by kind permission.

Printed in Great Britain

OXFORD UNIVERSITY PRESS, MUSIC DEPARTMENT, GREAT CLARENDON STREET, OXFORD OX2 6DP

The Moral Rights of the Composer have been asserted. Photocopying this copyright material is ILLEGAL.

9
mp
waits to be found when you're not ex - pect - ing to slip through the rab - bit hole
mp
waits to be found when you're not ex - pect - ing to slip through the rab - bit hole
mp
12
once more. Yes - ter - day,
p
once more. Yes - ter - day,
p
p
15
S. 1
oh yes - ter - day. Be -
mp
S. 2
oh yes - ter - day, yes - ter - day,
A.
oh yes - ter - day, oh yes - - ter -

18
-hind the hea - vi - est ward - robe door you might find yes - ter - day's
mp
oh yes - ter - day, yes - ter -
-day, yes - ter -
mp
mp
21
mf
sum - mer land. The play - ground dreams of hap - pi - ness where your
mf
- day. The play - ground dreams of hap - pi - ness where your
mf
- day. The play - ground dreams of hap - pi - ness where your
mf

24
unis.
mp
S. 1
S. 2
mo-ther al - ways holds your hand. Yes-ter - day,
A.
mo-ther al - ways holds your hand. Yes-ter - day,
mp
28
yes - ter - day.
mf
oh yes - ter - day, yes - ter - day. If
oh yes - ter - day, oh yes - ter - day. If
31
me - mo - ry ev - er de - serts the house, breaks the mir - ror and
me - mo - ry ev - er de - serts the house, breaks the mir - ror and
mf

34
leaves us a - lone, they say we'll not know right from wrong, we'll
leaves us a - lone, they say we'll not know right from wrong, we'll
37
mp
p
not know friend from foe. Oh yes - ter - day,
mp
p
not know friend from foe. Oh yes - ter - day,
mp
p
41
yes - ter - day.
oh yes - ter - day, yes - ter - day.
oh yes - ter - day, oh yes - ter - day.

44
più dolce
Yes - ter - day hides in your re - flec - tion, or just be - tween the gaps
più dolce
Yes - ter - day hides in your re - flec - tion, or just be - tween the gaps
più dolce
47
mp
in the floor, waits to be found when you're not ex - pect - ing to
mp
in the floor, waits to be found when you're not ex - pect - ing to
mp
50
slip through the rab - bit hole once more. Yes - ter - day,
slip through the rab - bit hole once more. Yes - ter - day,

53
p
oh yes - - ter - day,
p
oh yes - - ter - day,
p
57
oh yes - ter - day, oh
oh yes - ter - day, oh
rit.
yes - ter - day,
60
pp
yes - ter - day, yes - ter - day, yes - ter - day.
pp
yes - ter - day, oh yes - - - ter - day.
rit.
pp

2. Today

Bright and positive ♩ = c.138
SOPRANO 1
SOPRANO 2
ALTO
Bright and positive ♩ = c.138
PIANO
mf
4
TUTTI VOICES
unis. mf
I spun to - day on my fin - ger, threw it to you.
7
You picked it up like a pen and wrote your

11
f
own rules, to - day. To -
14
S. 1
S. 2
-day and to - day, and to - day, to - day and to - day, and to - day,
A.
-day and to - day, and to - day, to - day and to - day, and to - day,
f
17
the day, the day is light, and youth is star-
the day, the day is light, and youth is star-

20
- light.
- light.
mf
23
TUTTI VOICES
unis. mf
The mon - ster un - der your bed wears your best
26
clothes.
The day, the day's a pro - mise from a
30
best friend, to - day.
To -
f

33
S. 1
S. 2
- day and to - day, and to - day, to - day and to - day, and to - day,
A.
- day and to - day, and to - day, to - day and to - day, and to - day,
f
36
the day, the day is light, and youth is star-
the day, the day is light, and youth is star-
39
- light.
- light.
mf

42
unis. mf
We dance in the light of yes - ter - day's star
mf
We dance in the light of yes - ter - day's star
45
to - day and to - day, we dance in the light of yes -
to - day and to - day, we dance in the light of yes -
48
- ter - day's star to - day and to - day, we
- ter - day's star to - day and to - day, we

51
dance in the light of yes - ter - day's star to - day, to - day and to - day.
dance in the light of yes - ter - day's star to - day, to - day and to - day.
54
The earth is young, the earth is young to - day,
The earth is young, the earth is young to - day,
57
f
is young to - day. To - day and to - day, and to - day,
f
is young to - day. To - day and to - day, and to - day,
f

60
to - day and to - day, and to - day, the
to - day and to - day, and to - day, the
63
day, the day is light and youth is star - light, star -
day, the day is light and youth is star - light, star -
66
ff
- light, the day, the day is light and youth is star - light.
ff
- light, the day, the day is light and youth is star - light.
ff

3. Tomorrow

Breezy ♩. = c.63
SOPRANO 1
SOPRANO 2
unis. mf
You don't
ALTO
mf
You don't
Breezy ♩. = c.63
PIANO
mf
5
have to be scared of to - mor - row. Catch the tune that's thrown your way.
have to be scared of to - mor - row. Catch the tune that's thrown your way.
9
f
You'll find you won't need to wor - ry, to - mor - row's song will find, will find its
f
You'll find you won't need to wor - ry, to - mor - row's song will find, will find its
f

13
unis.
shape, to - mor - row.
shape, to - mor - row. It's
mf
17
mf
to be sung, to - mor - row, to -
some - thing a - bout to be sung or said, the whole world on the
mf
20
- mor - row. A tune that creeps from your mouth to the dance, a
tip, the tip of your tongue, to the dance, to -

23
S. 1
vel - vet seat in a glit - ter - ing room, to - mor - row.
S. 1
vel - vet seat in a glit - ter - ing room, to - mor - row.
A.
-mor - row, to - mor - row, to - mor - row. You don't
f
27
mf
ah
ah
have to be scared of to - mor - row. Catch the tune that's thrown your way.

31
unis.
f
S. 1
S. 2
You'll find you won't need to wor - ry, to - mor - row's song will find, will find its
A.
You'll find you won't need to wor - ry, to - mor - row's song will find, will find its
35
shape, to - mor - row.
shape, to - mor - row.
mf
Just
39
mf
as it comes, to - mor - row, to -
play each day as it comes to your head, strum - ming the fu - ture till
mf

42
- mor - row, and when the band, the band packs up, you
mid - night, mid - night looms, they'll be back to -
45
S. 1
know they'll be back, you know they'll be back to - mor - row. You don't
S. 2
know they'll be back, you know they'll be back to - mor - row. You don't
A.
-mor - row, to - mor - row, to - mor - row. You don't
f

49
have to be scared of to - mor - row. Catch the tune that's
have to be scared of to - mor - row. Catch the tune that's
have to be scared of to - mor - row. Catch the tune that's
52
unis.
S. 1
S. 2
thrown your way. You'll find you won't need to wor - ry, to -
A.
thrown your way. You'll find you won't need to wor - ry, to -
55
-mor - row's song will find, will find its shape, to -
-mor - row's song will find, will find its shape, to -

59
-mor - row.
-mor - row.
mf
63
p
oo
oo
p
oo
mp
Now it's mid - night and the moon writes down to - mor - row's tides.
mp

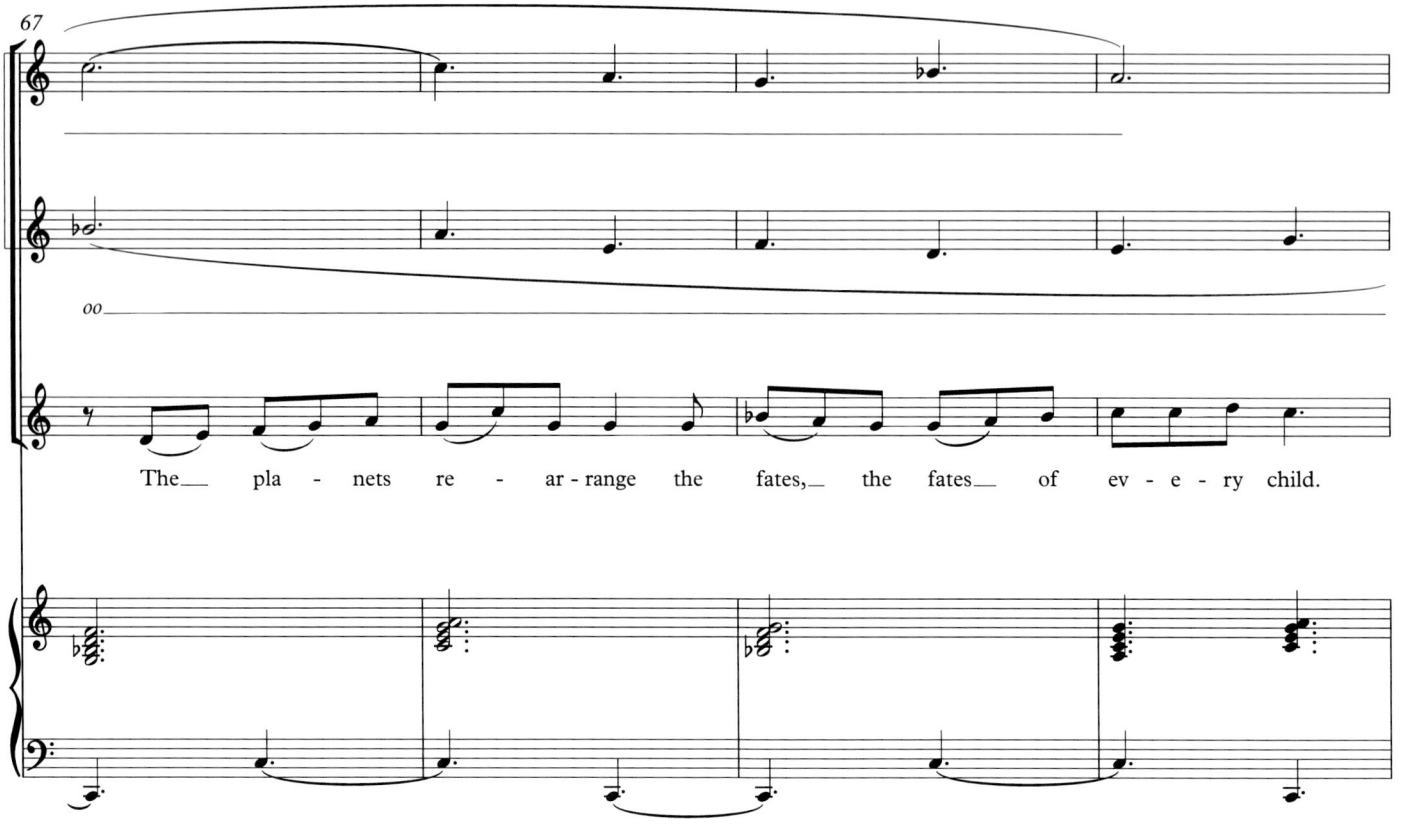
67
oo
The pla - nets re - ar - range the fates, the fates of ev - e - ry child.

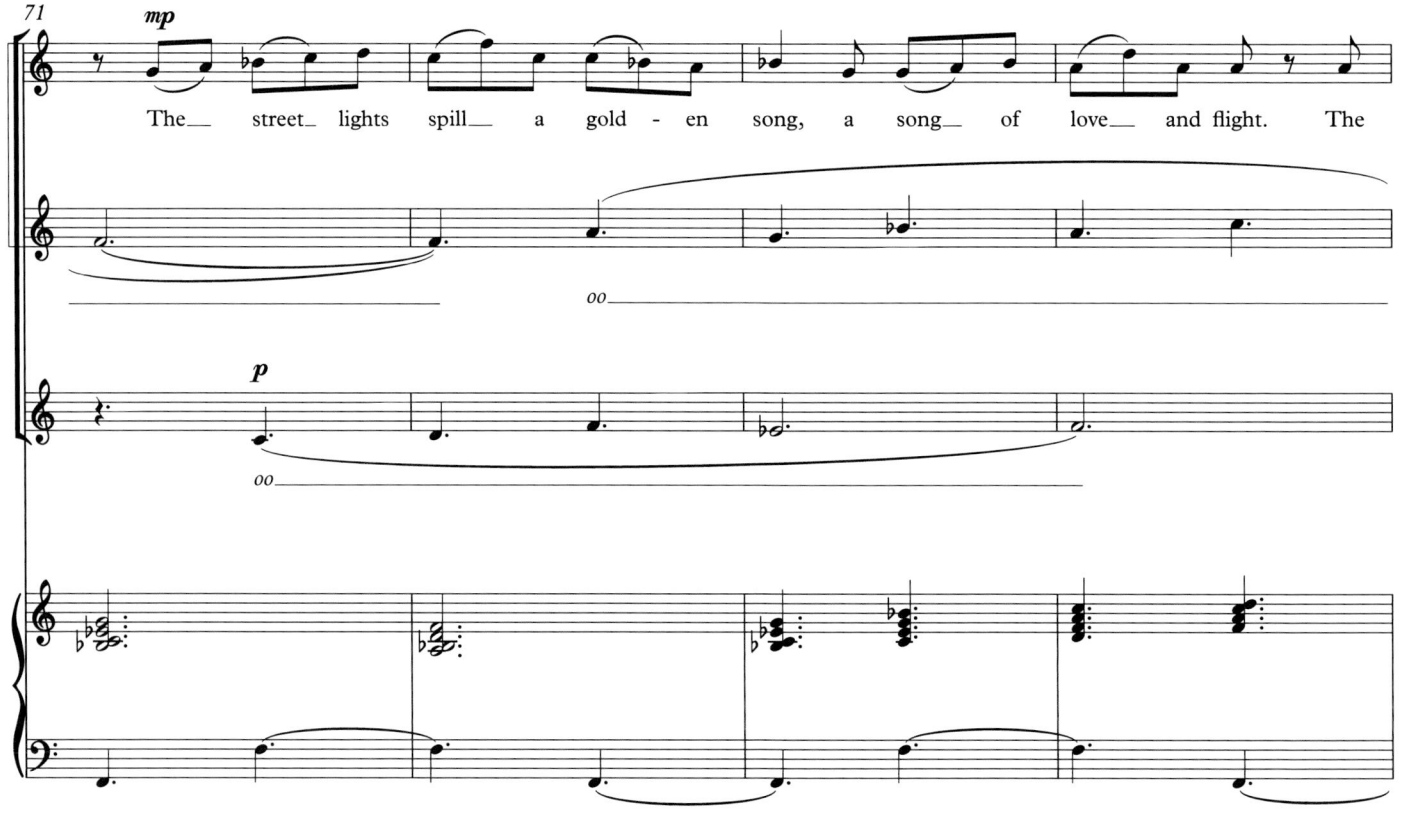
71
mp
The street lights spill a gold - en song, a song of love and flight. The
oo
p
oo

75
u - ni - verse is wait - ting for you to join the dots be -
mp
to join the dots be -
mp
oo for you to join the dots be -
78
f
-tween the stars to - mor - row. You don't
f
-tween the stars to - mor - row. You don't
f
-tween the stars to - mor - row. You don't
f

81
have to be scared of to - mor - row. Catch the tune that's
have to be scared of to - mor - row. Catch the tune that's
have to be scared of to - mor - row. Catch the tune that's

84
thrown your way. You'll find you won't need to wor - ry, to -
thrown your way. You'll find you won't need to wor - ry, to -
thrown your way. You'll find you won't need to wor - ry, to -

87
-mor - row's song will find its shape, to - mor - row.
-mor - row's song will find its shape, to - mor - row.
-mor - row's song will find its shape, to - mor - row. You don't
91
mf
ah
mf
ah
have to be scared of to - mor - row. Catch the tune that's thrown your way.

95
f
You'll find you won't need to wor - ry, to - mor - row's song will
f
You'll find you won't need to wor - ry, to - mor - row's song will
You'll find you won't need to wor - ry, to - mor - row's song will
2
2
98
find, will find its shape, to - mor - row, to -
find, will find its shape, to - mor - row, to -
find, will find its shape, to - mor - row, to -
2
2
2
2

101
-mor - row's song will find, will find its shape, to -
-mor - row's song will find, will find its shape, to -
-mor - row's song will find, will find its shape, to -
105
ff
-mor - row, to - mor - row, to - mor - row.
ff
-mor - row, to - mor - row, to - mor - row.
ff
-mor - row, to - mor - row, to - mor - row.
ff
fff